MARTIN LUTHER:
Man of God

Morton A. Schroeder

ILLUSTRATED by HAROLD SCHMITZ and HAROLD PAULSEN

Northwestern Publishing House

Library of Congress Card 83-60999
Northwestern Publishing House
3624 W. North Ave., Milwaukee, WI 53208-0902
© 1983 by Northwestern Publishing House, All rights reserved
Published 1983
Printed in the United States of America
ISBN 0-8100-0165-9

for Bettie

CONTENTS

Preface

This modest book had its origin in the imagination of the late Herbert R. Schaefer. Then general manager of Northwestern Publishing House — and factotum in charge of almost everything — Mr. Schaefer asked me to write vignettes on the life of Dr. Martin Luther. Simultaneously self-sufficient and yet part of a larger series of 48 designed to span the church year, each of the vignettes was to provide educational and inspirational reading material on the back page of Sunday service bulletins. During the course of the writing, Mr. Schaefer provided advice and counsel and a core Luther library. The series was published and met with some degree of enthusiasm. I was, and still am, grateful to Mr. Schaefer for his considerate treatment and help.

One of the present associate editors of Northwestern Publishing House, John A. Trapp, encouraged me to rework the material for publication during this anniversary year. While shepherding the book through its many production stages, Editor Trapp has been most helpful in matters concerning technical style and fluency of phrase. His contribution is large, and I thank him.

Although I have never met the artists who illustrated the book, I appreciate deeply their efforts to reproduce in picture the air and aura of a bygone day.

I also want to thank some of my colleagues on the faculty of Dr. Martin Luther College. Thinking they were answering general, conversational questions, they were in reality answering questions of fact, usage, style, and convention. Should they read this book, they will recognize their imprint.

I especially want to acknowledge the marriage-long assistance of my wife Bettie. Her faith in my ability to write a readable sentence has never wavered. She has encouraged me to write and to teach others to write. I will never be able to show her the depth of my appreciation.

All of these people — named and unnamed — are to be thanked for whatever merit this book has. I only am responsible for its faults.

Morton A. Schroeder
New Ulm, Minnesota
March 23, 1983

A Man of God

High on the honor roll of the world's great men stands the name of Doctor Martin Luther — a name cherished and loved by many, but hated and despised by those who stubbornly reject the gospel of Christ. Whatever else has been said or written of him, this verdict still stands: Luther was a man of God.

This simple peasant became God's tool to drive away the black clouds of the papacy and to restore the bright light of the gospel of Jesus Christ. All who saw him go about his calling saw a man they would long remember.

The black, deep-set, shining eyes flashed with the fire of an Old Testament Isaiah delivering the judgment of God against blasphemous Sennacherib as Luther strode through the streets of Wittenberg on that October 31, 1517, to post his ninety-five sentences on the door of the castle church.

The ears, layered with light-brown hair and lying close to a massive head, listened with the intensity of a Moses receiving the law as Luther caught the questions put to him by Romanist John Eck at the Leipzig Debate.

And at the Diet of Worms Luther's kind but firm mouth spoke in a clear tenor voice with the authority of a John the Baptist calling men to repentance. "I can or will recant nothing. . . . God help me. Amen." It was clear to all who heard that here was a man who, by the grace of God, would do great things. Yes, even Emperor Charles V had braced himself the moment before Luther entered the room. "I will never let that monk make a heretic out of me," he whispered to his attendant. The emperor had to suppress his fear that the bold professor standing before him might indeed be a man of God.

Martin Luther

A Child Was Born

Almost every American school child knows that Christopher Columbus discovered America on October 12, 1492. But how many know of that far more significant event which took place in a small German village just nine years before the great explorer found our land?

On the night of November 10, 1483, between the hours of eleven and twelve, a child was born by flickering lamp light to simple German parents. The infant's birth gave joy then only to his parents and a few friends and close relatives, but he was destined to gladden the hearts of Christians throughout the world and down through the centuries.

Baptized Martin Luther on the next morning, according to the custom of the time, in the nearby Church of St. Peter, this tiny child was to become a very special man of God.

Martin Luther was born in Eisleben, Germany. Eisleben, nestled at the foot of the Hartz Mountains, was a typical Middle Age town. The streets were crooked, narrow, and unsanitary. Walls surrounded the town and protected the inhabitants from attack. And no structure in the vicinity cast a longer shadow than the twin spires of the village church.

The house in which Luther was born stands at the head of the street which today proudly bears his name. Its roof was pitched high and was, in all probability, covered with red tile. The windows were filled with horn instead of glass, and the floor was made simply of dirt.

It was in this village, in this house, in a comparatively large room, that a child was born.

The Lord had a special calling for this child. During his sixty-three years he was to bring God's people back to the knowledge of God's Word.

Luther's Birthplace

School Days

Hans and Margarethe Luther lived in Eisleben until Martin was six months old. They then moved to Mansfeld on the banks of the Wipper River. Tree-covered bluffs rose above the town. The redstone castle of the counts of Mansfeld added beauty to the scene.

The copper-rich hills convinced Hans Luther that he could better his station here. Beginning as a simple miner, he became owner of two smelting furnaces and co-owner of six ore shafts. He bought a house, and here he and Margarethe raised their family and lived for the rest of their lives.

When Martin was still a small child, his father took him to the village school. The Luthers lived in the lower section of the town, while the school was in the upper part. This made school attendance difficult during bad weather, for the streets that ran up the hills were steep and slippery. Hans Luther was determined to give his son a better education than he himself had had. He often carried Martin to school in his arms. Sometimes an older boy would carry him on his back. This same boy later married one of Martin's sisters.

What did Martin learn in school? Religion held a prominent place. The children memorized the Commandments, Creed, Lord's Prayer, Ave Maria, hymns, and prayers to saints. Reading, writing, singing, and Latin were also taught. Latin was spoken, and all memorizing was done in that language.

The teachers were harsh, and they ruled with a heavy hand. Luther once was whipped fifteen times in a single forenoon for failing to learn a lesson that was not assigned to him. Later he wrote: "The preceptors were unskilled and as cruel as the hangman."

The Lord was using even these school days, which Martin described as "hell and purgatory," to train his servant for the task ahead — to prepare him as a preacher of the gospel, to the salvation of many souls.

Training for the Task Ahead

The Heart of a Woman

Hans Luther had big plans for his son: he was to be a lawyer, a man of influence. To accomplish this, he sent Martin to the Brethren of the Common Life School in Magdeburg, a city of 40,000 on the Elbe River.

Martin was not happy in Magdeburg. On one occasion there he fell sick with a high fever. It left him only when he broke all the medical rules of the day by drinking large amounts of water.

Father Hans learned that things were not going well for his son. Before a year was over, he withdrew him and enrolled him in St. George's School in Eisenach.

Eisenach, located at the foot of the Wartburg, was Margarethe Luther's native city. Her relatives received Martin gladly, but they were evidently too poor to give him the help he needed. He became a "crumb-seeker." "Crumb-seekers" were poor students who tried to support themselves by singing from door to door. Villagers gave them food, clothing, and shelter.

Martin had a fine singing voice, and this talent caught the attention of Ursula Cotta, the wife of a town councilor. She had heard Martin singing in church. She was also impressed with his attitude. One day when some singers came to her house, she singled out Martin and asked him to stay with her family.

In the home of Frau Cotta Martin began a new life. Treated as a son and surrounded with culture, he knew unbounded joy. He responded to this kindness by making rapid progress in school, and he surpassed the other boys in his class.

When Luther looked back on these happy days, he referred to Eisenach as "that dear city." Of Frau Cotta he said, "There is nothing sweeter on earth than the heart of a woman in which piety dwells."

The "Crumb-seeker" at Frau Cotta's Door

Which Father?

Hans Luther was overjoyed. His beloved Martin, from whom he expected so much, had received his master of arts degree. How proudly the parents accepted the congratulations of friends and relatives as they walked through Mansfeld.

And now Martin would continue his university studies. He would study law, and soon he would be a lawyer. Perhaps he could win the confidence of a prince and acquire wealth and honor. To make his studies easier, Hans gave him a set of very expensive law books called the *Corpus Juris*.

How did Martin feel? He tried to make his father's dreams come true, but his heart was heavy. He did not respect the profession. More than that, he was not at peace with God. Still unanswered was the question: What must I do to be saved?

Two events happened that made Martin overthrow his father's plans and take a step that changed the course of his life.

One of his acquaintances was found murdered in his bed. Martin was horror-filled at the thought that this sinner had died so quickly he had had no chance to prepare for death. What happened to his soul?

The second incident involved Martin directly. Returning to Erfurt in the summer of 1505, after a brief visit with his family, he was caught in a violent thunderstorm. The heavens were torn asunder. The wind roared. A lightning bolt struck near him, and as he fell to the ground, he cried out: "Help me, dear St. Anne. I will become a monk."

Two weeks later, Martin invited some friends to a party and announced his intentions, "Today you will see me and then nevermore."

Martin Luther, caught between respect for his earthly father and fear of his heavenly Father, had decided how to answer the question, which father? He thought his answer would help him find peace for his sin-burdened soul. But peace was not at hand.

"I will become a monk!"

Trust in Him

Martin Luther fulfilled his vow to St. Anne on July 17, 1505, by entering the Black Cloister in Erfurt. His decision, made in spite of his father's adamant objections and the pleas of friends, was based on his desire to please God. He said, "I made the vow for the salvation of my soul. I entered the spiritual state . . . to serve God and please him."

Life in the monastery was an ordeal. The strict daily schedule, which had to be kept in every detail, was made more difficult by the determination of the monks to show Martin that he was no better than they. The meanest tasks became his: he chopped wood, scrubbed floors, dug ditches, and carried garbage. When he begged on the streets, he suffered the taunts of former acquaintances. He added to his misery by fasting until he fainted from hunger and by whipping himself until his flesh bled. His cell became a torture chamber.

Martin was accepted into the Augustinian Order after his novitiate, or probationary period, was completed. Accepting the threefold vow of chastity, poverty, and obedience, he turned to the Scriptures with renewed curiosity and was ordained into the priesthood in 1507.

And yet he was not at peace. The more he read his own Bible and the ponderous Book in the monastery library, the more he felt he was not reaching the goal of holiness toward which he was striving.

But God did not give him more than he could bear. During one of Martin's deepest fits of melancholy, Dr. John Staupitz, a vicar-general of the Augustinian Order, said to him: "Throw yourself into the Redeemer's arms. Trust in him."

Martin Luther ultimately understood these words. He stopped trying to earn salvation by his works. He learned to know Christ as his Savior. He learned to trust in him.

"Sin was my torment night and day."

The Holy City

Advancement came quickly to Martin Luther. Eighteen months after he was ordained priest, he was called to the University of Wittenberg to teach. Vicar-general Staupitz must have had confidence in the brilliant young monk, for he was not yet twenty-five years old.

Martin was kept busy at Wittenberg. He lectured four times a week, led student discussions three evenings a week, and preached. This work did not keep him from his own studies, and he was awarded his first theological degree in March, 1509. Seven months later he returned to Erfurt. There he lectured on Lombard's *Sentences* to a small group of student monks assigned to him by the prior.

A controversy had been brewing in the Augustinian Order for some time. When it came to a head in 1510, John von Mecheln was chosen to lay the matter before the authorities in Rome. Martin Luther was appointed his traveling companion.

The long journey to Rome was made on foot, and the winter of 1510-1511 was severe. But Martin did not mind. Each passing day brought him nearer to his goal. When he saw it he cried out, "Hail, thou holy Rome, hail!"

December was spent in visiting holy places: churches, ruins, cloisters, catacombs, shrines, the "staircase of Pilate," and others. Martin was, as he said later, a "foolish pilgrim" hoping to win the forgiveness of sins with his visits.

But he was shocked with the ungodliness and filth he found in the Holy City. The priests lived in open lewdness and vice. They performed their duties carelessly and thoughtlessly. The "foolish pilgrim" was glad, nonetheless, that he saw these things. He said, "I would not take a hundred thousand gulden not to have seen Rome." Martin Luther could now preach and write of the brand of holiness he himself had witnessed in that city.

The Foolish Pilgrim

"He Must Make a Fuss"

The people of Wittenberg were used to seeing black-robed monks walk their streets. They paid little attention to the two who hurried away from the Black Cloister around noon on October 31, 1517. Had they known that Martin Luther was about to speak out against indulgences, they might have followed them.

Accompanied by his attendant, John Schneider of Eisleben, Luther ascended the steps of the castle church and nailed his theses to the north door. Few heard the actual blows, but their echoes resounded across Europe and called the faithful back to Christ.

Much had happened to Luther since his trip to Rome. He had returned to Wittenberg in the summer of 1511. Less than a year later, he was elected sub-prior of the Black Cloister and regent of the monastery school. He became a doctor of theology in 1512. Soon thereafter, he began lecturing at the university. In 1515, he was made district vicar and assistant in the town church. The silent years, 1511 to 1517, were busy ones. Luther, in writing of them, said in a playful mood, "You see how idle I am!"

Humanly speaking, Luther had everything to lose by posting his ninety-five sentences. November 1st was a great Roman Catholic festival, and thousands streaming to church already on Hallowe'en, the day before, would see what he had written. The learned would challenge him to prove his arguments. His superiors and many influential men would disapprove. He could be deprived of his positions, and his years of study could all come to naught.

But Martin Luther sought no personal gain. He was interested only in what the Scriptures had revealed to him about indulgences: they are contrary to God's Word! Poet Arthur Clough was right when he wrote of Luther: "He must forsooth make a fuss and distend his huge Wittenberg lungs . . ." so that man could know the truth.

Striking a Blow for the Truth

Ashes-Flesh-Bones

Martin Luther wrestled with the indulgence problem long before he posted his theses on the castle church door on October 31, 1517. As long as a year before, he had pointed out their evils. In sermons and letters, he showed his listeners that they could not buy loved ones out of purgatory with indulgences. He explained to them that their hope of purchasing the forgiveness of sins was folly.

His warnings went unheeded. Peasant and prince flocked to the indulgence fairs, which steadily increased near Wittenberg.

The pope needed funds to support himself in worldly luxury and to continue the rebuilding of St. Peter's Church in Rome. Founded by Constantine in 313, it had gradually fallen into disrepair. Pope Nicholas V began to rebuild it in 1450, and Pope Julius II rebuilt the basilica in 1506. Pope Leo X wanted to continue the project.

The church was completed in 1626. That it was expensive is easy to see. Visitors to Rome still marvel at its great size. It is almost 700 feet long, and the distance from the pavement to the eye in the lantern atop the dome measures over 434 feet. The structure covers over 163,000 square feet.

Luther was still a son of Rome. He thought the pope would discontinue paying for this work with indulgences. Accordingly, he wrote in thesis number fifty, "If the pope knew the exactions of the preachers of indulgences, he would rather have St. Peter's Church in ashes than have it built with the flesh and bones of his sheep ."

Brother Martin did not know Father Leo — this worldly blasphemer who once had said, "What an immense sum have we made out of this fable of Christ." He had no intention of calling his indulgence-peddlers home. He meant to have "the flesh and bones of his sheep" so that St. Peter's would be in gold, not in ashes!

St. Peter's Cathedral
A Monument to Papal Indulgences

I Absolve You —

The pope's plan to rebuild St. Peter's by selling indulgences did not meet with approval everywhere. Several countries refused to be taxed in this manner. Emperor Maximilian I, however, yielded to Leo's demands. Germany was divided into three districts, and Elector Albert of Brandenburg was appointed manager of one of them. John Tetzel, a Dominican monk, was Albert's chief salesman.

John Tetzel was born in Saxony and educated at Leipzig University. He began to sell indulgences in 1504. His career must have been successful; thereafter he was almost constantly peddling this merchandise.

Tetzel approached his victims with great pomp. The papal bull proclaiming the indulgence was exhibited on a velvet and gold cloth. Priests, monks, councilors, teachers, and common people formed a great procession and escorted him to the church. A red cross and the papal flag were set up while bells pealed and organs played. In front of the cross stood a large iron chest.

Gifted with eloquent speech, Tetzel played on his listeners' fears. He promised lavish gifts in return for a few coins: "Come, come, will you not invest ten, five, or a quarter gulden to get remission of all your sins and freedom from the terrors of purgatory?"

For all his knavery, Tetzel was not rash enough to invade Saxony. Elector Frederick had forbidden him to sell indulgences in his realm. But Tetzel, not to be denied, set up a fair at Jüterbock, just across the Saxon border. Luther himself tells us that "great multitudes ran from Wittenberg to buy indulgences."

When Luther became a doctor of theology, he promised "allegiance to my beloved Bible, to preach it faithfully and purely." He kept his vow by preaching, by writing to Prince Albert and asking him to recall Tetzel, and by posting his ninety-five theses.

Thus did he combat the indulgences of John Tetzel, which promised, "I absolve you from all sins and misdeeds, and remit all punishment for ten days."

"As soon as the money clinks in the chest
The soul flies up to its heavenly rest."

God's Mysterious Way

The reformation story is full of the name of Elector Frederick the Wise of Saxony. This powerful prince became Luther's benefactor, and in time of storm he stood between Luther and the papacy. The relationship between these two is an example of William Cowper's hymn, "God Moves in a Mysterious Way." It is true that Frederick befriended Luther, but for a variety of apparent reasons.

The University of Wittenberg was founded and partially supported by the elector so that his realm could have a school to rival the University of Leipzig. Frederick paid Luther's expenses in taking his doctor's degree only on condition that "for the rest of his life, Martinus would be responsible for the lectureship on the Bible."

When John Tetzel began to sell indulgences for Albert, the elector forbade him to sell in Saxony because he did not want the money of his subjects to flow into Albert's treasury.

Luther's safety became a grave matter to Frederick after the pope, realizing that the theses were not "a mere monkish squabble," commanded Luther to appear in Rome in 1518. Frederick would not permit his ablest professor to fall into enemy hands. The pope changed his plans and ordered Cardinal Cajetan to meet Luther in Augsburg. Frederick rejected Cajetan's demand to send Luther to Rome in chains. And he ignored the pope's letters calling Luther a "son of perdition."

The elector even had Luther kidnapped after the Diet of Worms. He realized that the safe-conduct promise, which he personally secured from the emperor, could be broken — especially after Luther was declared an outlaw. When Luther left his refuge in the Wartburg, Frederick permitted him to teach, thus defying both pope and emperor.

Frederick the Wise placed himself in danger by supporting Luther, and before he died in 1525, he took Holy Communion in both kinds, professing his belief in those doctrines which he had protected, in God's mysterious way.

Frederick the Wise

The First Victory

Martin Luther did not realize how popular his ninety-five theses would become. Nor did anyone else who lived in 1517. But they spread far and wide. Printed in German without Luther's knowledge, they "ran throughout all Germany" and spilled across its borders.

Friends praised the doctor for his stand, and colleagues who felt as he did came to his side. They knew that he spoke the truth, but it was up to him to broadcast it, since they were afraid to "bell the cat."

Luther's enemies reacted violently. John Tetzel boasted, "Within three weeks I'll have the heretic thrown into the fire." Dr. John Eck, a professor from Ingolstadt and former friend of Luther, attacked the theses in a pamphlet called *Obelisks*. Luther dubbed it a "hellish dose" and answered with *Asterisks*, a pamphlet of his own. Others joined the grim chorus, and Luther's friends began to fear for his life. The pope was not alarmed when he originally heard of Luther. Sometime later he ordered Luther's superiors to make Luther recant, but nothing came of it.

So matters stood for about nine months. When the "mere monkish squabble" did not diminish, Leo commanded Luther to appear in Rome to answer charges of heresy. When Elector Frederick would not permit Luther to leave Germany, Cardinal Cajetan, the papal representative in Germany, agreed to meet with Luther at Augsburg. The two met there on October 12, 1518.

Cajetan arrogantly refused to discuss Luther's theses. He simply demanded that the "shabby little friar" recant. Stormy sessions followed, but Luther refused to admit he had erred. Finally, the cardinal bellowed, "Recant! or never appear before me again!" Luther did not recant. He departed secretly and under cover of night, for he knew his life was in danger.

The cardinal had made his demands, but God gave his servant, the man with "deep eyes and queer speculations in his head," the strength to resist. His was the victory in this first battle with the papacy.

"Recant! or never appear before me again!"

One More Link

Cardinal Cajetan was in a rage. In a letter to Elector Frederick, he demanded that Luther be sent to Rome in chains. Frederick, in spite of the Golden Rose which the pope had bestowed upon him, would hear nothing of it. He wanted fair play for his professor.

Luther had to be silenced, Rome decided. And Charles von Miltitz took up the task. When he met Luther in Altenburg, Germany, he made no mention of the ban and interdict he carried. Instead, he denounced Tetzel as the cause of all the trouble. To Luther he gave embraces, kisses, and hypocritical lies. With tear-filled eyes he asked Luther to say no more. Luther agreed, on the condition his enemies remain silent, too. In January, 1519 the indulgence controversy seemed to be over.

God had other plans. The same Dr. Eck who had denounced Luther's theses attacked Luther again. This time it was on the pretext of answering Professor Carlstadt, Luther's friend and colleague. The promise of silence was broken; Luther felt free to speak. Eck had thrown the gauntlet; Luther took up the challenge — a debate was inevitable.

The handsome hall of Pleissenburg Castle was chosen as the scene of the debate. A tall, square-chested, self-confident Eck debated with a haggard and emaciated, but clear-voiced and eloquent, Luther. Dr. Carlstadt, who had been injured in a fall from his wagon, was ineffective in the debates, and after a while Luther took his place. Two hundred armed students and a few professors were all the assurance he had that the world had not turned against him. Eck, on the other hand, was honored in every way possible by university, city, and church officials.

The three debated from June 27 to July 15. Luther, now fully convinced that Rome preferred church fathers and council decrees to Christ, defended his teachings ably from the Scriptures. Eck was confident that he was the victor, but he did not realize then that one more link in the chain of papal darkness had been broken in the Leipzig Debate by the frail friar from Wittenberg.

His Defense: The Holy Scriptures

The Ties Are Broken

Dr. John Eck remained in Leipzig to socialize, to write learned opinions (as he described it), and to preach. He even wrote Frederick, urging him to disown Luther. Eck left on July 26 in the retinue of Duke George of Saxony, Luther's bitter enemy. Annaberg and Ingolstadt received Eck as a hero, but when he reached Augsburg he found that his attack on Luther had backfired.

Luther probably left the day after the debate, arriving home on July 20. He resumed his duties as pastor, professor, and writer. He published sixteen pieces, besides his *Commentary on Galatians*, within six months after returning. Of his efforts, he wrote: "I have a swift hand and a quick memory. When I write, it just flows out; I do not have to press and squeeze." These are not a braggart's words, for at another time, he said, "My own books . . . are themselves a sort of rude, undigested chaos." Nor did Luther want people to follow him blindly. "What is the use of making many books and yet always staying away from the chief book?"

Many of these writings answered enemies' attacks. Luther now turned to the more serious work of uncovering Catholicism's basic errors. *The Address to the Christian Nobility* appeared in August, 1520, and 4,000 copies were sold in eighteen days. Luther declared that the popes had "built three walls about themselves behind which they have defended themselves till now." Luther destroyed these walls and proposed thirty reforms to better man's spiritual and temporal estates.

On the Babylonian Captivity, which appeared in October, attacked the heart of papal error, the seven sacraments. The third paper, *The Treatise on Christian Liberty*, appeared in November. In it Luther described the meaning of faith and showed the sum total of Christian living.

These three earnest documents were Martin Luther's battle cry of freedom. No longer did he consider himself Leo's son. The ties were broken — completely and forever — between Wittenberg and Rome.

Three Letters to Free the Souls of Men

Bonfire at Elster Gate

On the morning of December 10, 1520, Philip Melanchthon announced one of the most dramatic acts in history by posting a placard on the door of the town church in Wittenberg. The notice invited "all friends of the truth of the gospel to be present at nine o'clock at the Chapel of the Holy Cross outside the walls, where the impious books of papal law and scholastic theology will be burned."

Shortly thereafter professors, students, and townspeople set out through Elster Gate for the town carrion-pit near the Elbe River. They carried books of Roman doctrine and writings of Catholic theologians. Wood was piled up and a fire was lighted. Volumes of papal error were tossed helter-skelter into the blaze by Luther's followers.

Martin Luther approached the fire. With trembling hands and a prayer on his lips, he cast in another document. "Because you have brought down the truth of God, may the Lord today bring you down in this fire," he said softly. For the moment only Martin Luther — and perhaps John Agricola — knew that he had burned the papal bull, the dreaded decree that branded him a "stiff-necked, notorious, damned heretic."

Six months before this, Rome had decided that Luther must be brought to task. Accordingly, the pope, after hearing John Eck's first-hand description of the heresy of the "beast of Wittenberg," had signed the bull on June 15. Dr. Eck was commissioned to carry it to Germany, where it was generally scorned and ridiculed. He did, however, manage to publish it in September. The bull demanded that Luther repent within sixty days or suffer the fury of the papacy. "Fury," of course, meant death.

It was this paper that caused Luther's books to be burned in Louvain and Liege. It was this paper that Luther ordered the pope to retract. Yes, it was this paper that Dr. Martin Luther, in a "pious spectacle," destroyed in a bonfire at Elster Gate.

The Bonfire at Elster Gate

My Mighty Fortress

Rome had her bonfire, too. On January 3, 1521, twenty-four days after Martin Luther had his bonfire at Elster Gate, the pope formally excommunicated him. To symbolize the deed, the Catholics in Rome gathered his books, carved a wooden statue of him, and burned them both in the *Piazza Navona*.

Charles V was in a predicament now. The newly-crowned emperor of the Holy Roman Empire, ruler of vast lands in both the Old and the New Worlds, planned to hold a diet at Worms, Germany. Empire problems were to be discussed at this meeting. One of these problems was the friar of Wittenberg, Martin Luther.

Elector Frederick the Wise, to whom the young emperor owed his new crown, urged that Luther be given a hearing at the diet. Only then, he argued, could he and his writings be judged rightly.

The pope demanded that Charles keep his vow to "defend the ancient faith." The Church had spoken; it was his duty to carry out her wishes.

Torn between the two, Charles wavered. First he invited Luther to appear at the diet; then he withdrew the invitation. Finally he granted Elector Frederick's request.

On March 26, the imperial herald delivered to Luther the emperor's citation to appear in Worms in 21 days. With the order came a promise of safe-conduct. Luther's friends reminded him of similar safe-conducts that had been broken in the past, but he quieted their fears with a simple "God will be with me."

Luther and three companions left Wittenberg in a two-wheeled, canvas-covered wagon on April 2. The 300-mile journey southwest across Germany resembled the march of a conquering hero. Crowds gathered everywhere to see and hear him.

Luther knew that God was with him. A prayer he offered in Worms shows again the simple faith that stood between him and despair: "O my God, stand by me in the name of Jesus Christ, who shall be my Shelter and my Shield, yes, my mighty Fortress. . . ."

"Lord, keep us steadfast in thy word."

Here I Stand!

It was Tuesday, April 16, 1521, and the good people of Worms were at their morning meal. Suddenly the trumpet blasts of the town watchman interrupted them. Two thousand of them dropped everything and hurried to the city gate. They knew that these blasts, reserved for important guests only, announced the coming of Dr. Martin Luther.

An impressive sight met their eyes. The cavalcade was led by the imperial herald. He carried the yellow and black banner of the Holy Roman Empire, and emblazoned on his chest was the imperial eagle. Luther followed him in the wagon. All along the way, friends and well-wishers had joined the train, until now it numbered over a hundred.

Luther entered the city and put up at the Knights of St. John House. There he received visitors until late into the night. Early the next morning, the imperial marshal delivered the royal order. He was to appear before the diet at four o'clock that afternoon.

At the appointed time, Luther stood before the mighty leaders of church and state. Emperor, electors, cardinals, bishops, and princes stared at the simple, black-robed monk who dared to argue with them. Two questions were put to Luther: "Are these books yours?" and "Will you retract them?" To the first, after examining the titles, he replied, "Yes." To the second, he said: "I beg you, give me time to think it over."

The late evening shadows were stretching across that warm and sultry second day, and the lighted candles cast an eerie glow when Luther, who had taken all to God in prayer, uttered his memorable reply, "Unless I am convinced by the testimonies of the Holy Scriptures or evident reason . . . , I am neither able nor willing to recant, since it is neither safe nor right to act against conscience. Here I stand; I cannot do otherwise. God help me. Amen."

Three private meetings followed, but Luther remained firm. By the grace of God he was convinced that his stand on the Bible was the right one. He would not recant. He would live the rest of his life and build the rest of his work on that stand which he had taken at Worms.

"Here I stand. I cannot do otherwise.
God help me. Amen."

Is Luther Dead?

Martin Luther was human, and a person can stand just so much. After ten days of arguments and conferences, he asked permission to leave. It was granted, along with a safe-conduct for twenty-one days.

The Luther party left Worms during the morning of April 26. Leading the group was the imperial herald who had brought the reformer to the diet. His presence gave Luther's friends little comfort. They remembered John Hus, who, together with his "safe-conduct," had gone up in flames.

Elector Frederick was proud of his professor, but he too was afraid. He said, "Dr. Martin spoke wonderfully before the emperor, but he is too daring for me."

The safe-conduct prohibited preaching on the way home, but Luther felt that this order was outside the power of the state. He preached whenever the opportunity arose.

When the party arrived in Eisenach, Luther received secret instructions to continue on less-traveled highways. Half the group went directly to Wittenberg, while Luther and two companions detoured to Moehra. There they spent the night with Luther's relatives. On the following day Luther's relatives accompanied him to Castle Altenstein. Night was falling when they turned back. Luther continued on through a narrow, tree-lined pass in the Thuringian Forest. Suddenly, without warning, four or five armed horsemen swooped down out of the woods and pulled him from the carriage. One of Luther's companions was so frightened he ran into the bushes along the road. The attackers, ignoring Amsdorf, Luther's other companion, disappeared as quickly as they had come. Luther was their captive. Where they took him, no one would say.

Albrecht Dürer, the great artist, spoke for all who loved the gospel. "O God, is Luther dead? Who will henceforth proclaim the gospel so clearly to us? O God, what might he not still have written for us in ten or twenty years!"

Kidnaped by Friends

The Land of Birds

Germany bristled with uncertainty after Luther's mysterious disappearance. Everywhere the questions were asked: Is Luther dead or alive? Where is he if he lives?

Charges flew thick and fast. The papists said Luther was hiding to escape just punishment. Luther's followers accused Rome of murdering him. And they had reason for this charge. The Romanists' opinion of Luther was well known. The Edict of Worms, published on May 26, said, "This devil in the habit of a monk has brought together ancient errors into one stinking puddle and has invented new ones."

The truth will out. The fact of the kidnapping gradually became known. It was Elector Frederick who had suggested the plan, but he did not know the details. He wanted to be able to tell Charles that he was ignorant of Luther's whereabouts.

After Luther had been seized, the party rode for hours in all directions, thus hoping to avoid pursuit. At eleven o'clock they reached a lofty height near Eisenach. On the summit stood an ancient fortress, its high walls forming an outline against the evening sky. The drawbridge was lowered, bolts were drawn, iron bars fell, and the gates opened. Martin Luther, completely exhausted, had reached the Wartburg Castle.

Long famous in legend and story, the Wartburg was set in a beautiful location. When Luther had attended school in Eisenach, he had seen its impressive towers looming above the Thuringian Forest. He had heard stories of the days when bold knights and gentle ladies graced its corridors. Little did he realize that some twenty years later he would be a captive within its crumbling walls. Nor could he have guessed that he would issue a German translation of the New Testament and several other important writings and pieces of correspondence from, as he would later name it, this Land of the Birds.

The Wartburg

Alone with God

Martin Luther was an unwilling guest in the Wartburg. He thought it was cowardly to hide while the fight raged on. "I did not want to come here," he wrote to a friend. "I wanted to be in the fray."

Nevertheless, he remained in hiding from May 4, 1521, until March 1, 1522. This ten-months' stay was broken only by a quick visit to Wittenberg in December, 1521.

The plan to keep Luther's identity secret was carried out in every detail. His monk's habit was exchanged for a riding costume complete with feathered hat, spurs, and rapier; lessons in knighthood replaced lecturing, and his beard was permitted to grow. Even his name was changed; Dr. Martinus became Knight George. His disguise was so complete that he was able to write to Melanchthon, "If you were to see me, you would take me for a soldier."

Knight George loved the quiet calm of his retreat. Walks through forest and mountain took some of his time, and once the castle warden included him in a hunting party. This was not to his liking. "There is some point," he said, "in tracking down bears, wolves, boars, and foxes, but why should one chase a harmless creature like a rabbit?"

Knight George became Martin Luther again in the privacy of his own two rooms, a sitting room and a bed room. "Far removed from people," the rooms could be reached only by climbing a back stairs. The Luther Room, which can be visited today, measures about twenty by fifteen by twelve feet. The furniture in the room today was not used by Luther, but he probably used some that was similar. From one of his windows, Luther could survey the rolling hills, and in the distance he could see smoke rising from charcoal-burners' pits. It was in this room that Luther spent many hours in study, meditation, and reflection. Here he completed some of his finest work, for here he was alone with God.

The Luther Room at the Wartburg

The Open Bible

One day in December, 1521, John Lang received a letter from the Land of Birds. It read in part, "I will remain hidden until Easter. In the meantime I intend to translate the New Testament into the language of the people."

With these simple words, Martin Luther announced the undertaking of his greatest task, the translation of the Bible into German.

Dr. Martinus set to work with amazing diligence, and his labors were crowned with signal success. When he returned to Wittenberg eleven short weeks after writing to Lang, he carried with him the complete translation of the New Testament. Dr. Reu says of this achievement, "Luther could not have accomplished it without the special assistance of the Holy Ghost."

Luther and Melanchthon began to polish the translation immediately. The presses started to roll in July, and it was published in September. It was a book of 222 pages, illustrated with fine woodcuts. A general introduction and an introduction to each book aided the reader. Even though the *September Testament* was very expensive, it became an immediate best-seller. One writer estimates that 200,000 copies were sold between 1522 and 1534.

Small parts of the Old Testament had been translated by Luther as early as 1517, but he now turned in earnest to the remainder. Learned scholars helped him, for he himself said of this task, "I acknowledge openly that I undertook too great a problem, especially in attempting to translate the Old Testament."

Because of difficulties in translating it, it was published in parts. The Pentateuch appeared in 1523, and thereafter sections were printed as they were finished. The first copies of the complete Luther translation were distributed by October 17, 1534.

Luther was never satisfied! He and his colleagues revised the translation to the day of his death. The last printed page on which he ever looked was a proof page from the 1546 revision of his translation of Genesis.

The Bible in the Language of the People

Make a Joyful Noise

Roman Catholics of Martin Luther's day were nothing more than quiet spectators during church services. They took little active part in the service; still less did they understand what was happening. The singing was done by the priests and the choirs. Congregational participation was restricted to chanting the *Kyrie* and certain responses. Only on feast days were the people permitted to sing hymns.

Martin Luther deplored the situation, for music was one of his early loves. "Music is a fair and lovely gift of God . . . ," he said. He wanted to share it with the people.

The problem was solved in Luther's characteristic fashion! He collected and revised existing spiritual songs, translated hymns from Latin, worked psalms into hymns, and wrote original compositions. He also encouraged friends like Spalatin and Speratus to undertake hymnwriting.

His work bore fruit. The first hymnal, a little pamphlet containing eight hymns, appeared in 1524. Four of the hymns were Luther's; three were by Speratus. The author of the eighth is unknown.

No sooner had this "tiny spring from which sprang the mighty stream of Protestant hymnody" appeared than the printing of Walther's *A Spiritual Hymn Book* was underway. It appeared in late summer of 1524. Twenty-four of the thirty-seven hymns were Luther's. Many other editions followed in rapid succession.

The papists groaned under this new attack. One of them lamented, "Luther's hymns have misled more souls than all his writings and sermons." Cardinal Cajetan said, "By his songs he has conquered us."

Martin Luther encouraged his listeners to use these songs. "See to it diligently that you learn and sing them better than you have sung in the past," he said. This man, condemned by church and state as an outlaw, wanted the church to be a singing church. And he did convince the people that they, with the psalmist, should "make a joyful noise unto the Lord."

The First Lutheran Hymnal

The Trumpet-Call

Johann Walther, master of song to the elector of Saxony, once wrote of his friend and co-worker, Martin Luther, "I spent many a pleasant hour singing with him and often found that he seemingly could not weary of singing or ever get enough of it."

That Luther "could not weary of singing" is easy to believe. He continued to write hymns for many years. By the time he died, in 1546, he had written thirty-six hymns.

Many of his hymns are sung the world over today. Every Christmas thousands of Christians sing "From Heaven Above to Earth I Come." At Pentecost like numbers join in "Come, Holy Ghost, God and Lord!" And who has not confessed his faith in the Trinity in "We All Believe in One True God"? No wonder Luther was called the Nightingale of Wittenberg.

Towering over all his hymns stands his most glorious composition, "A Mighty Fortress Is Our God." For years people have expressed their faith in God in its inspiring, triumphant words. Martin Luther based this hymn on Psalm 46, in which the psalmist declares, "God is our refuge and strength, a very present help in trouble." With this as his theme, Luther wove a message that breathes undaunted courage, the courage which he expressed when he said, "Even though there should be as many devils in Worms as shingles on the rooftops, I still would enter."

It is strange that the composition date of this hymn is unknown. However, it is believed that he wrote it sometime between the summer of 1527 and the spring of 1528.

Koestlin, an eminent Luther biographer, has succeeded more admirably than most in trying to describe the mighty melody and the heroic words that make up "A Mighty Fortress Is Our God." He wrote of it, "This hymn is Luther in song. It is pitched in the very key of the man. Rugged and great, trustful in God, and confident, it was the trumpet-call of the Reformation."

"A Mighty Fortress Is Our God!"

A Common Service

"I am glad that Wittenberg is flourishing," wrote Martin Luther from his Wartburg retreat when he heard of changes that were being made in his city.

His joy was short-lived. Under the leadership of Professor Carlstadt and monk Zwilling the people grew confused. Mob violence began; vandalism reigned. Images, pictures, and crucifixes were destroyed. Three laymen from Zwickau, who claimed to be "prophets of the Lord," incited the masses further. Melanchthon, unable to check the fanaticism, confessed, "The dam has broken, and I cannot stem the waters."

Luther felt duty-bound to return to Wittenberg. For eight days he preached, reminding his flock that force could not replace the Word of God. One of his listeners said, "He is daily pointing us poor, deluded men back again to the way of truth." Carlstadt's radical changes were abolished, and the old order of service was reestablished. Luther wanted to dispel the idea that outward changes in the form of worship were the main thing.

Luther knew, however, that some changes were needed in the church service, and so he began to revise it. His Latin order of service, *Formula Missae*, appeared in 1523. This was not satisfactory, for the common man could not understand it. The *German Mass* appeared in 1525. It was the Common Service in all its main parts as we have it today. The word "Mass" was purposely kept to show the people that a *new* communion had not been made, but that the Mass of apostolic days had been returned.

Unnecessary ceremonies fell by the wayside; the sermon recovered its rightful place; and congregational participation in song, prayer, and confession began. Above all, the service became Christ-centered: all parts of the Roman Mass which recalled Christ's redemptive work remained; those that stressed man's works were discarded. And the Sacrament was no longer to be considered a sacrifice which the priest offered to God, but as that sacred meal which Christ offered to his people for the forgiveness of sins.

A Common Service for the People

The Jewel of the Reformation

"The mere monkish squabble" refused to die. For almost twelve years its hammer blows had struck at error, finally breaking the papacy's hold on the people. Martin Luther had accomplished much since he had posted his theses on the castle church door. The gospel had been proclaimed in sermons and letters, the New Testament was in German, and the people had songs to sing.

One thing was lacking — well-instructed pastors who could preach and teach adults and children alike. In order to find out how conditions were, Luther and others visited churches and schools in Saxony during the winter of 1528-29. He wrote, "The deplorable condition which I recently observed when I, too, was a visitor, has forced and urged me to prepare this catechism."

Luther had thought of a catechism many years before, but press of work kept him from writing one. "I am postponing the catechism, as I would like to finish everything at one time in one work." He had even set others at the task. "Jonas and Agricola have been instructed to prepare a catechism for children."

The church visitation convinced him that the undertaking could be postponed no longer. He wrote in January, 1529, "I am busy preparing the catechism for the ignorant heathen." His labors again were blessed. Poster editions, convenient for use in the classroom, appeared first. The Large Catechism appeared in book form in April and the Small Catechism a month later. Both were illustrated with woodcuts.

Luther marked the results: "Tender youth are growing up well versed in the catechism and the Scriptures. . . . Thanks to this simple instruction, the youth of Saxony now understand the Bible better than the monks and nuns under the papacy."

Luther himself rated his catechisms above all his other writings. And for nearly five centuries, Christians throughout the world have hailed his Small Catechism as "the Jewel of the Reformation."

A Book for Children of All Ages

We Must Have Schools

Schools there were in Martin Luther's day. Cloister, Latin, German, and village schools offered an education to some young boys in Germany. Their condition was, however, unsatisfactory. Luther wrote about them, "We see how the schools are deteriorating throughout Germany."

This could not continue, Luther declared, for "the right instruction of youth is a matter in which Christ and all the world are concerned." He showed his personal concern by publishing his first major educational treatise in 1524, *The Letter to the Mayors and Aldermen of All the Cities of Germany in Behalf of Christian Schools.* Luther gave these three reasons for supporting Christian schools: 1) "In this work we are fighting against the devil, the most artful and dangerous enemy of men." 2) "We should not receive the grace of God in vain, and neglect the present favorable time." 3) "God's command given through Moses so often urges and enjoins that parents instruct their children."

Luther's second great educational treatise appeared six years later. In *The Sermon on the Duty of Sending Children to School*, the reformer explained the spiritual and the temporal benefits of education: "God needs pastors, preachers, and school teachers in his spiritual kingdom, and you can provide them...." He continued, "You can serve your sovereign or country better by training children than by building castles and cities and collecting treasures from the whole earth."

Luther's ideas about an educational system to care for all, regardless of sex or age, can be gleaned from these and other of his writings. All of his thoughts are important — even today. But over all stands his central theme: Education must be Christ-centered! "Where the Holy Scriptures do not rule," he said, "there I advise no one to send his son." He also said, "Above all, in schools of all kinds the chief and common lesson should be the Scriptures."

God bestowed many blessings on his people through Martin Luther, but few are greater than the one which stems from his determined declaration, "We must have schools."

"We must have schools!"

Thus Saith the Lord

The peasants of Germany were unhappy. For centuries they had suffered the hardships placed upon them by the papacy and the nobility, and many of them were little more than slaves. But now feudalism, the established order of the times, was crumbling. And the peasants wanted freedom.

Some of the peasants, working for better conditions, drew up twelve suggestions for reform. They sent them to Luther, hoping to win him to their side. They were sure he was for them. Had he not told the nobles, "Men will not and cannot tolerate your tyranny and arrogance much longer"? And did not the "evangelical liberty" which he preached give them the right to demand changes?

Before Luther could reply, violence broke out. Peasants, led by fanatics and radicals, murdered and robbed and plundered. Thomas Muenzer incited them to still more violence by urging them not to "allow their swords to cool from blood."

Martin Luther had favored some of the peasants' requests, but he wanted no part of this lawlessness. To him, anarchy was worse than tyranny. "Christians," he said, "do not fight for themselves with the sword and with guns, but with the cross and with suffering."

Returning from an attempted peace-making trip through the country, Luther wrote *Against the Robbing and Murdering Band of Peasants*. Part of it read, "If the peasant is in open rebellion, then he is outside the law of God." The tract urged that the rebellion be put down with force.

Unfortunately, this paper did not appear until sometime in June, 1525, after the peasants had been decisively defeated. It seemed as though Luther were kicking them when they were down. That is not true. Martin Luther had studied the problem in the light of the Scriptures and had scolded both peasant and prince for their crimes. His answer to the problem lay in Romans 13:1-4. He could say with confidence, "Thus saith the Lord."

Evangelical Liberty —
Not Violence and Rebellion

The Dream of a Prince

The whole idea was that of Jacob Sturm, a member of the city council of Strassburg. He and Martin Bucer, a pastor in Strassburg, thought it would be wise for the German and the Swiss groups who opposed the papacy to form a political union. A united front, they reasoned, would aid them in their struggle against the pope and the emperor.

Landgrave Philip of Hesse was approached, and the plan won his instant support. He tried to enlist the aid of other German princes, but he soon discovered that Elector John of Saxony, new to his position, would join no such alliance without Luther's consent. And Luther would agree only if doctrinal agreement were reached. Philip decided that the two groups should meet to settle their differences.

The castle in Marburg was chosen as the site for the conference. Here in October, 1529, Martin Luther met Ulrich Zwingli, the Swiss leader. Zwingli was pastor of a reformed church in Zurich, Switzerland.

Fifteen points were discussed in this meeting, but on the last vital point of doctrine they reached an impasse. Zwingli taught that the body and blood of Christ were not truly present in the Lord's Supper. To Zwingli it seemed more reasonable to call it merely a symbolical meal. The bread and wine, he said, only represent Christ's body and blood.

Martin Luther met reason with the Word of God. Standing before a large square table, he cast aside the heavy, deep-colored Persian rug which served as a tablecloth and pointed to four words which he had written in chalk on the oak surface: THIS IS MY BODY. He clung to these words of Christ and refused to have their meaning changed in any way.

Luther would not tolerate Roman error; neither would he permit Zwinglian falsehood. He said to the Swiss group, "I cannot consider you as brothers until you grow wiser on this point of the Sacrament." As for Philip of Hesse? He knew that in those four words the dream of a prince had come to an end.

"This is my body!"

Hours in Prayer

The Marburg Conference was over. Truth had triumphed, and Landgrave Philip's plan of union without doctrinal agreement had failed. Danger to the gospel now arose from another direction. Emperor Charles V, having solved some of his political problems, renewed his attack on Luther's alleged heresy. He invited the Lutherans to come to the Diet of Augsburg in the spring of 1530.

The summons to appear at the diet before the imperial legislature, written in friendly terms, deceived the Lutherans. They left Wittenberg with the hope of getting a fair hearing. Elector John of Saxony and others joined the original group along the way. They traveled together, arriving at Coburg Castle on Good Friday, April 16.

Martin Luther was disappointed when the party set out for Augsburg, for he was left behind. He was still under the imperial ban, and his life would have been in danger had he left friendly soil.

Even though Luther was 150 miles from Augsburg, he guided his followers in all their actions. His time was spent writing and receiving letters, reading drafts of confessional articles, and giving advice, comfort, and courage. He wrote to Melanchthon, "If I hear that matters are going wrong or badly for you, I will hardly be able to constrain myself, and not fly over to you, to see how horribly Satan's teeth do bite." Illness and the news of his father's death added to the burden he carried.

Martin Luther knew how to "take it to the Lord in prayer." He prayed, "I know that you remain our Father and our God. Therefore I am certain that you will confound those who persecute your children. If you do not do it, the danger is yours as well as ours. For the entire matter is your own."

And God, who has commanded his children to "pray without ceasing," could not refuse this man, of whom we have heard, "Not a day passes in which he does not spend at least three hours in prayer."

A Man of Prayer

Also Before Kings

Martin Luther remained within the protective walls of Coburg Castle, but the gospel of Jesus Christ marched forward. On May 2, 1530, the Lutheran delegation arrived in Augsburg. Emperor Charles V kept them waiting; he did not enter the city until six weeks later.

Knowing now that they would not get a fair hearing, the Lutherans changed their plans. The original defense of Luther and the electors of Saxony was broadened and enlarged into an "all-embracing confession." The task fell to Melanchthon. Using confessional articles that Luther had written previously, he and other Lutheran theologians labored mightily to prepare a document that would present their case ably and well.

Luther was informed of all the changes, and correspondence between Coburg and Augsburg quickened as the confession neared completion. Melanchthon requested that Luther "give judgment on the whole writing." Luther replied, "I have read the Apology of M. Philip. It pleases me right well, and I do not know what to improve or change in it; neither would it be proper, for I cannot tread so gently and quietly."

On Saturday, June 25, at three o'clock in the afternoon, the diet gathered in a large front room in the palace of the bishop of Augsburg. Emperor Charles V mounted his throne, and the electoral chancellors, Dr. Brueck and Dr. Beyer, stepped forward. Dr. Beyer read the German copy, loud enough so that his voice carried beyond the 200 in the room to the throngs gathered in the halls and courtyard. When he finished, after two hours of reading, the assembly knew that this confession — The Augsburg Confession — spoke for those who were "within the Scriptures."

Luther was jubilant. He wrote, "I am overjoyed to be living at this hour when Christ is openly confessed by so many in a great public assembly and with so good a confession."

And to this great public confession, Martin Luther applied the words of Psalm 119:46, "I will speak of your testimonies also before kings, and will not be ashamed."

The Augsburg Confession

"Nothing But Heaven"

The year 1518 was hardly the least eventful of Martin Luther's many event-filled years. Because Luther had posted his theses, the pope commanded him to appear in Rome. Because he had dared to dispute too vehemently with Cardinal Cajetan, he had to flee for his life. And so on. But one bright ray broke this otherwise gloomy scene — on August 25, Philip Melanchthon came to Wittenberg.

Philip Melanchthon was born with the family name of Schwarzerd on February 14, 1497, to a skilled master-armorer and his wife. He was not an imposing figure. Luther referred often to his "delicate frame" and on one occasion jokingly called him a "scrawny shrimp." He had a hitch in his shoulder and a defect in his speech. His manner was timid, and his health was poor.

But Melanchthon's mental gifts more than made up for his physical weaknesses. He did outstanding work in school as a boy, and he became a high school teacher at seventeen. His inaugural speech at Wittenberg, made when he was only twenty-one, so impressed the older professors that they worried about losing him. Luther himself wrote, "I hear that the Leipzig people are already boasting of their power to take him from us."

Coupled with his scholarship was devotion to duty. So hard did he work that Luther had to caution him, "God can be honored not alone by work but also by rest and relaxation." His diligence bore fruit. Luther wrote to Spalatin, "His lecture room is always full!" In fact, as a university lecturer, he was more popular than Luther.

Philip Melanchthon became Luther's intimate co-worker and lifelong friend. He helped Luther translate the Bible, and he assisted him in visiting churches and schools and in founding new schools. Besides this, Magister Philip stood shoulder to shoulder with his colleague at Leipzig, Marburg, and Augsburg.

Philip Melanchthon's chief weakness was his urgent desire to compromise. After Luther died, "the little Greek" yielded too much where he should have yielded nothing. But his dying wish was that of a devout and sincere child of God: "Nothing but Heaven."

Philip Melanchthon

The Power of God

"Dr. Staupitz, you are killing me. I'll die in three months." So said Martin Luther when he was asked to preach his first sermon. Luther's fears of the pulpit were real. He said: "I feared the pulpit, but I had to mount it. They forced me to preach. I had at least fifteen arguments with which I wanted to refuse Dr. Staupitz."

Luther never overcame the awful weight of this duty. In later life he said, "Believe me, preaching is not something men can perform in their own power; for though I now am an old and experienced preacher, I nonetheless am fearful when I am to preach."

This fear did not keep Luther from preaching God's word. How many sermons he delivered is unknown, but 2,300 of them are still in existence, their themes covering everything from the grandeur of angels to the greediness of swine. In the year 1528 alone, he preached 195 sermons in a period of 145 days.

Luther's contemporaries give us a vivid picture of Luther, the preacher in the pulpit. He was energetic and earnest, his eyes flashed and sparkled, his voice was vibrant with the urgency of the message. One listener wrote, "Everyone who hears him once desires to hear him again and again, such tenacious hooks does he fix in the minds of his hearers."

It is easy to understand why Luther held his hearers' attention. His introductions were short, he stayed with his text, and he did not parade his learning. Above all, he gave to his office the dignity and the reverence which he felt for it. "There is," he said, "no dearer treasure nor any more precious thing on earth or in this life than a real and faithful pastor or preacher." To him these words of the Apostle Paul had real meaning: "For the preaching of the cross is foolishness to those who are perishing; but to us who are saved it is the power of God."

Luther the Preacher

A Suitable Helper

The vow that Martin Luther took when he became a monk included the promise never to marry. The Scriptures, however, showed him the error of making such a promise, and he did not feel obliged to keep it.

As early as 1519 he said, "Oh, truly a noble, great, holy estate is matrimony." Later he encouraged priests to marry, quoting 1 Timothy 3:2 as his authority, and he showed that monks and nuns had the same freedom. He said some time later, "I am exceptionally pleased with the marriages of the priests, monks, and nuns."

Luther himself was not inclined to marry. He wrote to a friend, "So long as I am in my present mood I shall not marry. Daily I await the death and punishment of the heretic."

But the urgings of friends and father — and his conviction that "celibacy is a devilish institution" — prompted him to "confirm by way of example" what he had taught. After taking his problem to God, he acted with surprising rapidity.

At five o'clock on the afternoon of June 13, 1525, Martin Luther took Katherine von Bora to be his wife. Present at the simple service in the Black Cloister in Wittenberg were Jonas, dean of the castle church; Bugenhagen, the pastor of the town church, who performed the ceremony; Dr. Apel, professor of law at the university; and the artist Lucas Cranach and his wife. Among the many guests present to "help pronounce the benediction" were aged Hans and Margarethe Luther.

Martin Luther once wrote, "They shall never force a wife on me." But he also wrote, "Take care lest it happen, for God is accustomed to do what one least expects." And God, in his own good time, did just that for his servant, Martin Luther. In Kate, God gave him a suitable helper indeed.

Luther's Marriage

Far Above Rubies

Leonard Koppe, a member of the Torgau city council, was a venerable gentleman of sixty years. No one would have suspected that his canvas-covered wagon carried anything but herring and other provisions for the Nimbschen convent. But this Easter eve in 1523 it was carrying a strange cargo. A group of nuns from the cloister filled the barrels on the return trip. One of the nuns was Katherine von Bora.

Katherine von Bora was born on January 29, 1499, in Lippendorf. Left motherless at a tender age, she was placed in the Nimbschen cloister when her father remarried. At the age of sixteen, she was consecrated a nun and accepted into the Cistercian Order.

The rumblings of the reformation gradually spread, and in due time Katherine and her sister nuns heard them, too. After reading smuggled copies of Luther's works and studying the Bible, they saw no reason for staying in the cloister. An escape plan was worked out, and the herring-barrel wagon did the rest.

The ex-nuns were placed in good homes and otherwise cared for by Luther and his friends. Katherine lived with the family of a prominent lawyer for a time and later with Lucas Cranach and his wife.

Martin Luther had no interest in spirited and ambitious Katherine at the time of her escape. After her first love had left Wittenberg, he even tried to match her with a friend. As God willed it, Luther was to be her "pious husband."

When Luther married Katherine, he wrote to a friend: "I am not passionately in love, but I esteem my wife." Years later he tuned his voice to sing a sweeter song: "I love my Kate; yes, I love her more than myself." At another time he said, "Kate, you are an empress." Twenty years of married life found Martin Luther asking frequently, "Who can find a virtuous woman?" Equally often he answered, in the words of Solomon, "Her price is far above rubies."

Katherine Luther

Union and Communion

"From that most gracious woman, my best of wives, I have received by the blessing of God a little son, Hans Luther, and by God's wonderful grace I have become a father." With these jubilant words, Martin Luther announced the arrival of his and Katherine's first child on June 7, 1526.

God blessed this marriage with five other children. Elizabeth died in her first year. Magdalena lived to be only thirteen. Martin studied theology, but ill health prevented him from entering the ministry. Paul became a successful doctor, holding the position of physician to the Saxon court. Margarethe married a wealthy nobleman, and her descendants live to the present time.

Luther's children were reared in a God-fearing atmosphere. The Bible was read, and catechism lessons, prayers, and Scripture verses were learned. Luther gave practical demonstration of his own teaching that a parent should "consider the child nothing less than a precious eternal treasure, entrusted to his protection by God."

Luther was firm with his children. He once refused to see Hans for three days, saying, "I would rather have a dead son than a disobedient and wicked son." According to the Reformer, however, "the apple ought to lie next to the rod." He told his children stories and fables. With them he played games, worked puzzles, sang songs. When he was away, he wrote letters; when he returned, he brought gifts. Once when he was in Torgau, he wrote to Kate, "Although it is market season here, I can find nothing for the children. Have something on hand if I should fail to bring something home for them."

Martin Luther's home life was relaxing, and a few hours with his family helped him to face difficult problems anew. No wonder he could say: "When truth and faith, children and fruits of love are there, and marriage is regarded as holy and divine, then indeed it is a blessed state. For the union and communion of man and wife are a great thing."

Luther with His Family

Tried in the Furnace

Tragedy was no stranger in the home of Katherine and Martin Luther. As God tried the heart of David, so he also tried his servant Martin Luther. But he did not give him more than he could bear.

Elizabeth Luther was born on December 7, 1527; less than eight months later she was dead. Luther and his wife were grief-stricken. Her death, Luther said, "left me with a strangely ill, almost effeminate, heart." He added, "Elizabeth bade us farewell to go to Christ, through death to life."

As the years passed, Luther's cup of happiness was filled to overflowing. The reformation was, under God, making gains, and people were returning to the gospel. The children now numbered five, and all were prospering under his and Katherine's care. And then death returned.

Magdalena, Luther's favorite child and special joy, suddenly became seriously ill. Brother Hans, at Torgau with his teacher, was summoned home at once. His sister was living when he arrived, but anxious days followed. Luther, beset with anguish, tried to comfort his wife. He said, "Dear Kate, remember where she came from. She is faring well."

When "little Lena" took a turn for the worse in late summer, Luther prayed, "I love her so dearly, but since it is your will, dear God, to call her away from here, I willingly let her go so that she may be with you." Turning to Magdalena, he asked: "Would you like to stay here with your father, or would you willingly go to your Father in heaven? " After replying, "Dear father, as God wills," Lena died in her father's arms.

As Magdalena was laid to rest, Luther said to the tearful crowd, "You ought to rejoice. I have sent a saint to heaven, yes, a living saint." Martin Luther knew that "all things work together for good to those who love God" — even being severely tried in the furnace of affliction.

Tried in the Furnace

A Message to Hans

Dr. Martin Luther wrote thousands of letters, but none is more beautiful than the one he wrote to four-year-old Hans. The place from which he wrote it was Coburg Castle; the time was June 19, 1530, a critical time for Luther, both as a man and as a reformer.

Being caged in a castle did not agree with energetic and dynamic Luther. He had been ill during his captivity in the Wartburg, and similar troubles bothered him again. Added to his sickness was his grief over the death of his father, whom he had hoped to see once more before he died.

Topping all this was his concern about the happenings at the Diet of Augsburg. The Augsburg Confession, now nearing completion, would soon be presented to the assembled princes of church and state. The thirty-man guard at the castle reminded him that, humanly speaking, the battle could be lost and he would have to be protected by arms against the fury of emperor and pope.

In spite of all these cares and worries, Luther took the time to write to his little son. Aside went the translation of the Old Testament, the editing of *Aesop's Fables*, and his theological letters and opinions. The result was one of the most engaging pieces of literature ever written.

Part of the letter reads, "I know a lovely, pleasant garden, in which there are many children. They wear golden jackets and gather nice apples under the trees, and pears, and purple and yellow plums. They sing and run. They are happy and have pretty little ponies with golden reins and silver saddles. Therefore, dear little Hans, learn and pray cheerfully; then you will come, together with your friends, into this lovely place."

Martin Luther was a man of wide learning, a profound thinker. Yet how easily he could shed his role as a theologian and scholar and become the playful father of a little child! This is evident in his message to Hans, a message full of childish fancy and imagination! Hans asked his mother to read it to him again and again.

"I know a lovely garden . . ."

A Man's Home

The Black Cloister in Wittenberg was more closely connected to Martin Luther's life than any other building in the Luther lands. There he lived from 1508 until the time of his death. The work of the reformation took him from it on occasion, but it was home to him for most of this time.

The Black Cloister was a three-story stone structure, measuring 165 feet by 45 feet by 40 feet. It lay on the banks of the Elbe River in the southeast corner of the town. Separating it from College Street, Wittenberg's main thoroughfare, was a spacious, tree-dotted lawn and flower garden enclosed by a brick wall. A gate, on either side of which was a small house, led into this courtyard. Behind the cloister, next to the city wall, was a vegetable garden where Luther puttered around for relaxation.

Many changes were needed to convert the cloister into a home. Two tons of plaster were used in the remodeling, and one hundred gulden, an electoral gift, provided some "new home necessities." The kitchen and the laundry were on the first floor. The second floor, reached by a spiral stone stairway, became the actual living quarters.

"Before I was married," Luther said, "the bed was not made for a whole year. I worked all day and was so tired at night that I fell into bed without knowing anything was amiss." The "Morning Star of Wittenberg," as Luther called Kate because she rose so early, changed all this. Floors were scrubbed, walls and ceilings were whitewashed or painted, flowers were planted. Luther described his wife's energy with no small pride. "She rides about, cultivates the fields, raises and buys cattle, and the like."

Received as a wedding gift from his prince and transformed by a woman's touch, this erstwhile dormitory for some forty monks became a man's home — where Martin Luther lived happily with his family.

The Black Cloister — Luther's Home

Gems of Wisdom

The five o'clock supper table that Katherine Luther set was like few others in history. Welcome at it were people from all walks of life; to it came friends, acquaintances and strangers from near and far, visiting pastors and professors, students, the tutors of the Luther children, Luther's own secretaries, and the like.

The conversation that spiced the meal and often continued into late evening was also different. Martin Luther, the head of the house, set the pace. Under him, the talk ranged from playful banter to serious doctrinal discussions. Everything imaginable, from the ridiculous to the sublime, had its inning: bees, birds, books; misers, marriage, mercy; freedom, faith, frogs. Nothing was too delicate or too trivial to evoke a comment from Luther.

Sometime in 1531, Conrad Cordatus decided to record Luther's remarks. Veit Dietrich, Luther's private secretary from 1529 to 1534, followed his example. Others were soon doing the same. Anton Lauterbach, who proved to be the most diligent, added a new angle: he improved his own notes by comparing them with others.

John Aurifaber, who trafficked in Luther memorabilia, got the idea of publishing them. This he did in 1566. His own notes are the poorest of the lot, for he was with Luther only during the last two years of Luther's life. He embellished his scanty record with the materials of others.

Table Talks, for so these conversations are called, are not reliable as historical source-material. There are too many probable misquotes. And remarks isolated from their context are always easy to misinterpret. They are, however, a valuable record of Luther the man. Listen to him: "Monks are fleas on God Almighty's fur coat." "One must hold fast to the Word." "Only let us pray, for the victory will not be won by arms or counsel, but only by prayer."

Not everything Luther said was worth saving, but from his lips there fell many gems of wisdom, all of which make us appreciate this great man of God all the more.

Table Talk

With Love, From Kate

Martin and money were soon parted. So generous was the reformer that he would have given away his last coin had he had the opportunity. Students, relatives, friends, and fair-weather companions knew he would grant their requests. And he never failed them. On one occasion, we are told, he gave away silverware that belonged to his children.

Not so with Kate! She was known throughout Wittenberg for her frugality. Luther himself said of her business-like ways, "What do I care if I am in debt? Kate pays the bills."

Katherine Luther had good reason to count every gulden. In addition to caring for her own family, she was responsible for feeding the many guests that regularly sat at her table. The near-dozen nieces and nephews whom she and Martin supported had to be fed and clothed, too. In fact, so many persons found their way to the Black Cloister that the third floor was made into living quarters.

She did well! Not only was she able to meet her own obligations, but she was also able to put away some money for a special occasion.

At Kate's request, Luther wrote to Pastor Lauterbach in Pirna about "a carved house-door." Kate included the measurements, and on November 10, 1540, she presented the portal to her husband. It is made of Pirna sandstone and, in the style of the time, has projections above that serve as canopies, and seats directly beneath. Carved above the seats are these inscriptions in Latin: "He lives," and "You are 57; in silence and in hope shall my strength be." Balancing each other on either side are carvings of Luther's bust and of his coat of arms.

Luther often spoke of his love for Kate. With this splendid gift, she expressed her love and affection for him. Every time the reformer left or entered his home, he was reminded that the "Katherine Portal" was given with love, from Kate.

The Katherine Portal

Into Eternity

Nearly half a millennium has passed since Dr. Martin Luther lived and labored to bring the gospel of Jesus Christ to fallen mankind, but present-day visitors to the Luther lands need not wonder where some of the most famous events took place. Monuments, tablets, and memorial markers of various kinds have been erected to preserve the memories.

Some of these tablets mark the location of structures that have long since crumbled into ruin. Others describe the buildings that have been restored by persons, societies, and governments who were, and in some cases still are, interested in preserving as much as possible of the path that Luther trod. Still others are attached to landmarks that have withstood the ravages of time.

One marker can be seen just outside the east end of Wittenberg. It identifies one particularly sturdy, stately oak as the Luther Oak. On the plaque are the words: "Dr. Martin Luther burned the papal bull at this place on December 10, 1520." An iron railing surrounds the tree to protect it from enthusiastic visitors who are tempted to take pieces of bark as souvenirs.

To the rear of the Luther Oak stands a grove of tall spruce and pine trees. White gravestones glisten at the feet of these trees. One of the graves is that of Luther's daughter Magdalena, buried near the site of one of the greatest triumphs of her father.

One very famous Luther scholar maintains that the Luther Oak does not mark the site of the burning of the bull. Be that as it may! The significance still remains. Just as the oak tree symbolizes dignity and strength and endurance, so Luther's bold deed symbolized the breaking of the powers of the Antichrist.

The Luther Oak will some day totter and fall. But the church of God, to which Martin Luther labored to return the erring, will last into eternity.

The Luther Oak

This Tells the Story

A seal or coat of arms is usually designed to commemorate an outstanding event or to express the hopes and ideals of the family or person who bears it. Each part of such an emblem has a special meaning.

Martin Luther's seal is no exception. As early as 1517, while Luther was professor at Wittenberg, he replaced his father's seal with one that he himself designed. Composed of five parts, it suited him better than did the crossbow and two roses of Hans Luther.

After Duke John Frederick had the seal cut in stone for a signet ring, Luther's friend Spengler, the town clerk of Nuremberg, asked for an explanation of it. Luther wrote to him, in part:

> The first thing expressed in my seal is a cross, black, to put me in mind that Christ crucified saves us. "For with the heart man believeth unto righteousness."

> Now, although the cross is black, mortified, and intended to cause pain, yet it does not change the color of the heart, does not destroy nature — that is, does not kill, but keeps alive. "For the just shall live by faith" — by faith in the Savior.

> This heart is fixed upon the center of a white rose, to show that faith causes joy, consolation, and peace. . . .

> This rose, moreover, is fixed in a sky-colored field to denote that such joy of faith . . . is but an earnest and beginning of heavenly joy to come. . . .

> And around this field is a golden ring, to signify that such joy in heaven is endless. . . .

Luther explained in detail his reasons for choosing certain colors and the significance of those colors. He also made comparisons between this life and the "bliss in heaven," which is "anticipated and held by hope, though not yet revealed." But brushing aside the details, the gist of the letter was simply this: The coat of arms tells the story of what I believe and confess.

Luther's Coat of Arms

Yes

Martin Luther was called upon to settle many complaints and grievances that did not fall within his duties as pastor, professor, and reformer. He himself said: "I daily receive so many letters that my table, my benches, stools, desks, windows, and shelves are full of inquiries, complaints, petitions, etc."

One such task arose when the counts of Mansfeld asked him to settle their quarrel. In spite of the fact that he was, in his own words, "old, decrepit, lazy, worn out, cold, and now one-eyed," he set out on the five-day journey to meet them in Eisleben during January, 1546.

Kate knew that her Martin was ill, and she worried about him. He wrote to her, "I have a better Provider than you and all the angels could be. Be therefore at ease. Pray and let him provide."

The dispute was settled peacefully on February 17, but the three weeks of bickering had proved too much for Luther's tired body. He became critically ill that same evening. During the night, periodic gains in strength were followed by severe relapses. He knew his sojourn on earth was near its end. To his sons and his friends he said, "Pray for our Lord and his holy gospel that its mission may be successful, for there are many who would hinder it."

Hot cloths relieved the pains in his chest for only a short time, and a stimulant soon lost its effect. In agony he cried out, "O Lord God, how I suffer! Dear Dr. Jonas, I believe I am going to remain here in Eisleben where I was born and baptized."

During his waking moments he recited Scripture passages, prayed, and three times commended his soul to God. When he could hardly speak any more, Dr. Jonas asked him: "Reverend father, will you die professing Christ and the doctrine you have preached?"

It was between two and three o'clock on the morning of February 18, 1546, that Martin Luther, in the presence of several witnesses, spoke his last word, "Yes!"

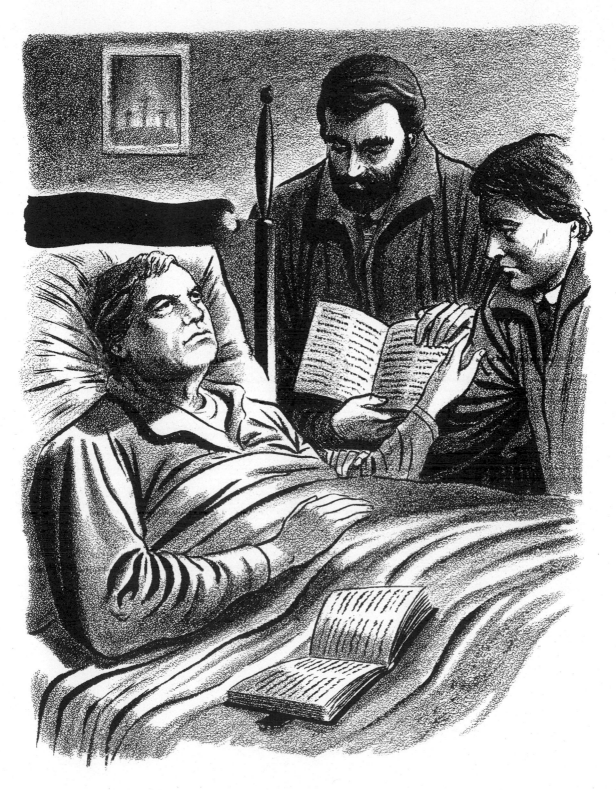

Luther's Death
February 18, 1546

I Have Kept the Faith

The news of Martin Luther's death spread rapidly into castles and cottages, and the rich and poor alike came to verify the report. The house in which the body lay became the focus of a milling, grief-stricken crowd.

A service was held on February 19, at two o'clock in the afternoon in St. Andrew's Church, just across the street from where Luther had died and only a few blocks from where he had been born. Luther's good friend Jonas delivered the sermon. Only a short time before, Luther had preached his last sermon from the same pulpit.

The counts of Mansfeld begged that Luther be buried in Eisleben, but Elector John refused their request. After a second service the following day, the funeral procession started out for Wittenberg. Tearful people met the train everywhere. In stunned silence, or with uncontrolled weeping, they followed along as far as they could.

At nine o'clock, on the morning of February 22, the procession reached Wittenberg and passed through the Elster Gate. The tolling of the bells floated on the air as the hearse made its way down College Street to the castle church. Two knights and sixty horsemen went before it. Carriages carrying the immediate family, other relatives, and dear friends followed. Professors, students, well-known Wittenbergers, and several thousand people came on behind.

During Pastor Bugenhagen's address both he and the congregation wept unashamedly. Melanchthon delivered the Latin address. For his text he chose Revelation 14:6-7. He identified Luther with the "angel . . . having the everlasting gospel," who said with a loud voice, "Fear God, and give glory to him." He also praised Luther as the greatest teacher in the church since the Apostle Paul.

Following the European custom of burying prominent people in church, the casket was lowered into a vault in front of the pulpit. The words which Paul wrote when death was near could now be said of Martin Luther: "I have fought a good fight, I have finished my course, I have kept the faith. . . ."

Luther's Burial Place

Jehovah-shammah

How Wittenberg appeared during Martin Luther's lifetime is not easy to imagine. One of Luther's friends called it "a poor, unsightly town with small, old, ugly, squat, wooden houses, more like an old village than a town."

There is some truth to this description. Wittenberg was only eight blocks long and four blocks wide. It had one main street and about 2,000 to 2,500 inhabitants. The town church, the castle, and the castle church were its only imposing structures.

In the castle church young Martin Luther became Dr. Martin Luther in 1512. To its north door he nailed his ninety-five theses. In it he heard his friend Melanchthon make his inaugural address as a faculty member of the university, and in it both he and Melanchthon were laid to rest.

The castle church was a stately building already during Luther's day, for Elector Frederick the Wise had almost finished his rebuilding of the original modest structure when Luther arrived in Wittenberg. It was designed by master architects and decorated by skilled artists. The nave was 100 feet high, 45 feet wide, and 160 feet long. The hills that rose in the distance provided a beautiful backdrop for the 200-foot main tower.

Time has left its marks on the castle church. It was partially destroyed on several occasions, and today it is quite different from what it was four hundred years ago.

The castle church was one of Romanism's fairest jewels in the early sixteenth century. Elector Frederick had converted it into a showplace for his collection of relics, numbering between 15,000 and 20,000 items. Pilgrims who viewed them — and made appropriate contributions — were rewarded by having their stay in purgatory shortened.

By the time Martin Luther died, the relics had long lost their significance to those who accepted the Word. Nor did purgatory have any terror for the child of God. Martin Luther could say of the church: The pope reigns no more. *Jehovah-shammah*, the Lord is there.

The Castle Church at Wittenberg

God Was His Anchor

An earnest young shepherd boy, unskilled in fighting and armed with only a sling, went forth one day to do battle with a giant that had killed many men. He was taunted and mocked and cursed. But he was not afraid. And when the battle was over, David the shepherd had conquered Goliath the giant. The Lord was on his side.

Hundreds of years later another David went out to fight another Goliath.

Martin Luther studied the Bible; he "searched the Scriptures." What he found made him realize that the religion of his fathers was false. Romanism had so perverted the gospel of Jesus Christ that people were being led far astray from that which makes us "wise unto salvation." The "lamp unto our feet" had been snuffed out; the blind were leading the blind.

All this Martin Luther saw. And such conditions, he knew, could not continue!

On October 31, 1517, Martin Luther posted his ninety-five theses on the castle church in Wittenberg, Germany. During the twenty-eight years of life that remained, he continued the unequal struggle. Together the pope and the emperor tried to crush him, to root out and to destroy him and what they regarded as his heresy. When the battle was over, they saw that they had failed.

Martin Luther accomplished what he did because the Lord was on his side. He alone could have done nothing. Luther knew this, and to his Lord he turned for constant help and counsel. Luther was a man of prayer. When seemingly insurmountable problems faced him, he turned to God. He pleaded and begged, and it sometimes sounded as though he were scolding. He knew that God was his "refuge and strength," his "strong tower," his "pure defense." Psalm 68:1 became his battle-cry: "Let God arise, let his enemies be scattered: let them also that hate him flee before him."

Philip Melanchthon said it well on the day when Luther was buried: "God was his anchor and his faith never failed him."

God Was His Anchor